Layers of Me

Karely Tlacoxolal

India | USA | UK

Presentation by *BookLeaf Publishing*

Web: www.bookleafpub.com

E-mail: info@bookleafpub.com

ISBN: 9789363301399

First edition 2024

This is for her, the little girl who has loved literature since she was in first grade. Special shout out to my first grade teacher Ms. Farinella who got me into my love for reading and made Read-Aloud such a fun part of the day! For my nieces and nephews, my motivation to be here. And to all my readers, you are much appreciated for giving me a chance to express myself to all of you.

ACKNOWLEDGEMENT

This book wouldn't exist without BookLeaf Publishing, and their constant encouragement and motivation to get to the finish line (finishing my very first masterpiece). Thank you BookLeaf Publishing!

PREFACE

Many of these poems come from my personal experiences, past and present. I talk about my loved ones and touch on God, since I am a believer of Him. My poems are intended for people who have gone through similar experiences growing up, women and girls that want to feel inspired and empowered and for everyone to feel motivated and connected with.

Peek-a-boo Heart

Thorns and barbwire,
A heart that's tired
Creates a gate
Zero pain
And separates
A face, a mask
You see, don't ask
Cold but warm,
A bipolar storm
Snow then rain,
Peace and pain
Outside you see
A serious face,
Her eyes intense,
Constant stress
Creates a gate
Zero pain
And separates

Laughs and smiles,
Her lifestyle
A beaming face,
Sunny days
Sparkling eyes,
A pair of twinkling lights,

Side by side,
A stellar sky.
Cozy cuddles like a bear,
Get a whiff of her hair,
Floral breeze of fresh air,
Blue like the ocean,
Waves in motion.

Eye rolls and disses,
But she yearns for
Hugs and kisses
Hope you read minds, we're
Two souls intertwined,
Mental telepathy,
Words spoken breathlessly,
Touch and caresses,
"He wants me", she guesses
"Me too", she confesses,
Clothes removed,
Both on the move
He accesses her body,
It becomes a hobby
With motions that impress,
They slowly decompress,
While each other's bodies they possess
But at the end of the night
We're both still a mess,
Thoughts are still repressed
They try to make it right.

Hands being held,
Makes her heart melt
A drug, an addiction
An exclusive edition
As she hopes they're both blessed
With love, healing, and success.

Miles and Memories

Every time I see that door
It reminds me that you're not here anymore

Nowhere to go now when I'm bored
Shut in my room, everything I ignore

You understood me to my core
But you're not here anymore

Nothing is like before
When will our family be restored?

God knows the times I've implored
Meanwhile my mind's a constant war

The day you come back my heart will soar
But for now
Everytime I see that door
It reminds me that you're not here anymore

Whispering Waves

5

Waves, come and go
On a journey, they run and flow
Full of highs and lows as we all know

Concealing their stories with each motion
Each time the tide returns from the ocean

Carrying magic, wishes and emotions
The water remains loyal to the land
Their bond is like an eternal love potion
Always comes back longing for sand.

The Muse of Tenacity

Fighting her own battles,
She stands tall,
No matter how many times she may fall.

She's got herself, needs no one else
Some call it pride, but she prefers to self-guide,
She now knows not to confide.

Continuing on the path she's paved,
Gave up on being saved
She never waivers or caves,
Her mother taught her to be brave.

Her spirit's unbroken,
The pressure is on but
Her resolve never gone.

In dark times when all seems lost,
The hero rises, no matter the cost.
A true warrior over all
Ready to answer when duty calls.

Little Blessings

Each one I listen to, the stories they tell
Where fits of laughter and love do swell

We chill, we hang, we giggle, we play
Each one has my heart in a special way

First came "Larry the little boy"
"Now too old to play with toys"
Gaming boy, obsessed with skins
Screams are loud when he wins
A heart so big and a diet like mine
Partners in crime, we get along fine
More than a nephew, a little friend,
He's like my bro, we do TikTok trends

Next comes Jayden, a mischievous rascal
With his character, sometimes a hassle
Nonetheless he spills much love
You just can never get enough
Might be a tough cookie for others
To me, with hugs and kisses he smothers
At times has a high little temper,
But his sweet words are so tender
His rare laugh's a melody that tinkles,
Like a cupcake topped with sprinkles

Then comes little Bella
Like a mini Cinderella
Locks of beautiful hair
Like all the love she spares
Her hands held together, forming a heart
I do it right back, a pair of sweethearts
Always puts a smile on my face
When she runs yelling hi like it's a race
She wonders and follows, she questions and
guesses
Like a small news reporter her questions are
endless

Soon after she comes in a hassle,
Her name's Milani but I call her my little rascal
With big round eyes, taught me to love mine
I lift her and carry her, we cuddle all the time
This past birthday just turned three,
Now she dances filled with glee
Kisses my forehead and my cheeks across
Gives me her blessing, forming a cross

Last but not least is little Jacob
He loves to explore in his own way
His little talk melts my heart each day
He spreads on the floor, he loves to lay
Reaching out with such small hands,
His tiny fingers hold mine tight

That little smile the room ignites
Loves to tickle and loves to play
He learns something new and I yell yay!

Titi, Tia, K!!
Hello, Guess what, Hooray!

Watching them grow brings bittersweet tears
As time passes by through the years
But the bond we share will never fade,
It can only grow stronger, here to stay
Little blessings that light up the scene
For a kiss or hug from them I feen
And I'll always support them with a cheer
For them, my love will never disappear.

Childhood Baggage

Don't ask me what is love?
If you're expecting an answer and I give you
another one
How am I supposed to know "what is love" if
I've never felt it given to me long enough
How should I know "what is love" when "my
first loves" turned their backs on me
I will forever ask if that love was ever there and
if it was is it still there?

I never felt a closeness to my dad, barely ever
felt his protective hand.
So how will I know when I feel safe, if I never
really felt that way
Mommy on the other hand was always there,
But that only made the wounds harder to repair
Her absence forever damaged my heart
My childhood years went falling apart.

For years I longed for some love from either one
But both were wrapped up with their new
number ones.

I don't wish to blame them for what I've gone
through,

All I need is acceptance for why my bad mood.
I now understand they were broken too,
Knowing that makes my soul blue

All that's left is for me to heal,
In hopes that one day I'll feel a love real

Whispers of Love

In a crowded room, he caught her eye,
Her heart beating fast, she couldn't deny

***

How can I not enjoy our time together I have to
confess I wish those moments could last forever
because I love when you grab me and we cuddle
while you mess up my hair and when you tickle
me and I have to hold it in pretending I don't
care. I love when you hold me so tight that it
makes me feel safe and so close I can smell your
delicious sweet smell and feel your heartbeat
like it's got somewhere to be except it's right
here touching me. I love when I sit on top of you
and I can play with that hair you say you hate
but I love so much and the big hugs that you
give me so strong you crack my back. I love
when you reassure me and you tell me it's ok,
you kiss me on my forehead and tell me to stay,
I love it so much it makes my day. I love when
you hold my hand while you drive especially
knowing you could've lost your life, it's like
you're keeping me safe and I do it right back,
always together staying on track. I love when

you hold my hand when we walk knowing damn
well if you don't I'll probably trip on the
sidewalk. I love when we make fun of each
other, when you tease me and I tease you right
back, I laugh uncontrollably until you pick me
up spontaneously and I scream begging you to
put me down slowly. I love it when you say I'm
adorable and only when you say it my smile is
uncontrollable. I love the nicknames you've
given me, the ones only you and I know about,
that no one else can call me cuz I'd ignore them
without a doubt. I love when you tell me "You
got this" when I get stressed, I love that we wish
each other luck on our tests, I love the way you
explain things to me I don't know, I love how
passionate you get and the patience you show..
The same patience that makes me feel safe and
relaxed when we are alone

***

Leaning against you, we look at each other's
eyes
You hold me tighter, your heart throbbing eager
for the prize

Unmatched and Unstoppable

No one's ever walked in my shoes so only I get
to choose.
Now watch me get the job done, you know how
I do

I do what I want wherever I want whenever I
want however I want and no one says anything
they know not to start.
If you ain't a collaborator that's fine just don't be
a traitor,
I pay no mind to the haters I'm too busy with my
labor.

I'm out here doing me if you choose not to
believe that's simply envy
They try to match me but they can't, sweetie you
will never be me,
They do one I do two and go as far as three
Don't care what's said no one's out here grinding
as hard as me.
Gets it all done she can't even catch a break
But she knows to keep going, her future is at
stake
I take no days off and if I do, I'm still getting my
money too.

I'm in the zone, working even on my phone
For many years I've been alone, no one's gonna
do it I gotta get myself that throne.
And whatever you think you know let me tell
you, you really don't
Just cuz I can run in your shoes doesn't mean
you can do what I do.
Even if you tried you could never walk in mine
So how about you go check yourself and realign
that mind.
If you wanna be in the game you gotta learn to
move the strings
I'm not here to play I'm here to take some wins.
If I feel like it I do it
If I want something I get it
If I crave something I pay it
And whatever I do I absolutely slay it
If you mad seeing me slay, I'm sorry what can I
say I work hard in my day to day.

Whoever criticizes probably got nothing to
pursue they out here all day looking for
something to do. They see you looking good and
they wanna be like you, just cuz I make it look
easy doesn't mean its true.

Keep it chill, just be you

No need to fake, just break through.
If you think you're better than me
Do the work and go check yourself,
Then come back and tell me if u still agree
I think there's something you might have forgot
You can't be better than something you're simply
not.
Sorry hun you can't run with me if you don't
know how to act
If I see you acting funny I'll just take a step
back.
I don't bother with fools I no longer waste my
time
I keep my distance just as long as you don't
bother me or mine.
May whatever people wish for me they get it
multiplied
I know whatever I do, I'm justified.

Don't forget to sow so you can reap
When this is over
That's all you'll get to keep
You must accept the fruit that you collect
It's what you planted
Now take in its effects.

Life's trials may try to bring her down
But she will forever hold onto her crown.

Child of God

God always comes through for me.
He calls me his little honeybee

When he's close I'm filled with glee
He's got the key to make me happy.

He's got my back, and all the tea
He lets me be, lets me be free

When I need him, I'm on my knees
After talking to him I feel in peace.

That is all I want, all I need
And God brings it to me.

He always comes through for me
There is no way to disagree.

Endless Love Song

18

And every time you miss me don't forget that I
am here
Though we may be far just know my love is
always near

I always pray to god to take care of you my dear,
Anything happening to you would be my biggest
fear

And just in case it still was not quite clear,
You will remain in my heart year after year

Sprinkles of Sunshine

I know it's going to be a good day when I
awaken and it's bright in my room but I'm not
sweating and uncomfortable in my bed. I feel
happy when the week is filled with sunny days
but not when the sun is beating down hard
making you sweat and feel irritated, more like
when it's warm and bright enough with a gentle
breeze that caresses your skin and brings you
relief. You know when you look up and it's a
vision of sky blue and cloud white, no darkness
in sight. I know it's going to be a good day when
I check my phone and there's a message from
my sister saying she's going to order breakfast
and if there's anything I want. I get happy when I
am home alone and I could dance to any TikTok
trend. I know it's going to be a good day when I
check my account and I got money to spend so I
get ready to go shop for clothes and so my
collection extends. I feel happy when I take the
time to get all cute and it pays off because I feel
good but what makes it even better is when older
women feel the need to compliment my look. I
know it's going to be a good day when I think I
won't catch the bus that's already at the bus stop
but the driver spots me crossing the street like

crazy and waits for me to make it. I get happy
when I'm about to walk in somewhere and a guy
is nice enough to open the door for me and let
me in first, I swear I appreciate it so much it
makes my heart burst. I know it's going to be a
good day when I'm walking down the streets,
playing music through my earphones pretending
I'm the star in a music video. I feel happy when
I'm in my little room alone savoring my mango
the way I love it and drinking my coconut water
in bed all chill, it's like my own little introvert
vacation. I know it's going to be a good day
when the little kids run up to me and hug me, the
more excited they are to see me, the more my
job feels dreamy. I get happy when I go to the
beach and I feel the cold water reach my feet, it's
at that very moment I feel complete. I know it's
been a good day when I've spent it laughing all
day and my belly is hurting but it's in a good
way, and all my troubles have been replaced by
pleasurable pain and tears in my eyes from
giggles I embrace. I know these good days will
not always remain, but they'll return soon in time
again for June.

Versions of Me

The elderly lady I helped when her groceries fell
off her wheelchair onto the sidewalk will tell
you I'm an angel sent from heaven. The old hags
who talked about my fam will tell you I'm a
disrespectful girl who knows only aggression.
The impolite guy who pushed past me on the bus
line is shocked I didn't let it slide and now stares
at me wide-eyed, so I stare right back until he
looks away and I comfortably recline. The flirty
gentleman who complimented me earlier is still
stealing glances while I try to look elsewhere,
with my hair my smile I hide because if he
catches it I can't bear. The little boy I played
basketball with thinks I'm fast and competitive
and fun to play around with. The little girl that
plays with my hair will tell you she wants to be
like me one day, that my hair is not a wig. My
mom might say I'm a lazy girl and wishes I did
more while my teachers will express how much
I strive to make all my grades soar. The one
that's insecure with her own body will question
me on mine and ask about my eating habits
meanwhile there's 10 other people suggesting
this doll becomes a model and to take a stab at
it. My dad might tell me I gotta grow up faster,

and be a little more responsible but the guys that
know my story will make me see that I'm pretty
independent and unstoppable. He said, she said,
they said, he thinks, she thinks, they think this
and that but only God and I know what I'm
really like, what's not, why's that and what's a
fact.

Chains of the Past

I try to move on but how can I start?
With so many days I feel my life fall apart
It always goes back to the same old event,
My soul is so damaged, it still has a dent
Even I'm tired of having to vent,
It seems like there's nothing much more to be
said

I know there's so much that I unpack
But day after day it keeps coming back,
So just let me be, I'll try not to slack,
Sometimes I just need a little pat on the back,
At the end of the day I still don't crack, you
won't even notice what I lack.
There's just one thing that I ask,

Please don't judge how I deal and dealt
With a pain and trauma you've never felt.

Loyalty's Legacy

She's a small place of trust, in a world full of crime.
Just watch yourself when it comes to any of mine,
The minute you act a stranger, all I see is danger, so don't step out of line.

It's loyalty that makes you my family
While blood simply my relative.
And the loyalty I receive is the one I will return,
The minute it's broken, the whole relationship burns
Because these are tested with stories untold or secrets not disclosed
No matter how much you want the tea, my mouth remains closed.
I always know who's a yes and who's a no.

People intently wait for you to slip up, I'm sorry you're low and I'm still up
They're looking to play me, and I remove myself like that's my cue
I just go bye, and looking back I be like phew!

She knows loyalty like hers is rare,

Which is why she always remains aware
But her loyalty runs deep in her veins, an
unspoken promise that forever remains.

In moments of darkness, when shadows loom
near, her loyalty shines bright, banishing fear.
For loyalty is not just a word or a vow, it's a
sacred promise that's honored here and now.
So let's raise a toast to those who stay true, to the
real ones who always see us through.

Because in a world full of temporary ties and
false friends, this loyal warrior stands strong till
the end.

Where Have You Gone?

Even when I didn't want to (go anywhere)
I was forced to go with you (everywhere)

Now I get to choose
And I am not forced to go with who knows who.

You didn't care for my mental state,
Your priority was your new mate.

Kind of like a caterpillar who went into the
cocoon,
And came out not ready, a little bit too soon

Or like a beautiful little flower who would have
blossomed into something more
But was ignorantly pulled out from the ground,
And she never got to grow into what her future
had in store

4 long years of my life have vanished,
Years I waited for my departure day to be
established.

I wish those years had given me better
experiences,

At least it taught me the true meaning of what
resilience is.

It's true what they say, the things you have to go
through shape you into who you are today,
I always have that in mind but looking back at
what I didn't get to do, I can't hide my dismay

Because it sucks so much to have so many
things I wish I did,
But at the moment I just don't have much time to
do

But I'll be sure to have fun in life now that I
finally have the control
There's nothing more in life that would make me
feel happy and more whole.

Soul-stirring Surge

The lights dim, everyone rises
My anxiety fades away and my energy arises

The beloved voice emerges from the speakers
All the fans scream in delight, they're keepers

The star pops out and the crowd goes wild
Thousands of faces lit up, big crazy smiles

Mid through the night you realize you'll
remember this forever
Kept in your heart, a memory you'll treasure
And you're ready to repeat the experience
whenever

Mismatched Freaks

I want someone that's going to match my freak
but not just once in a while, I need it at least
once a week. I gotta warn you this is not for the
weak but if you're down please tell me now
because you're going to need to speak my
language and by that I mean my TikTok
language so that when I make a TikTok
reference you get it and you don't think I'm
making no sense and you take no offense. Are
you going to listen to me complain about being
tired all day then proceed to stay up together all
over again? Are we going to watch horror
movies even if I get scared and you'll probably
have to follow me in the house everywhere? Are
we going to sleep not just together but
surrounded by all my stuffed animals and a
blanket even if it's not winter that we can share?
Are you going to watch me talk to myself in the
mirror and not think I'm delulu but join me
because it's nothing new? Are we going to read
the same book so we can talk about if after and
pretend we're the main characters of the book so
we can act out scenes and call each other new
names?
Is somebody gonna match my freak?

Are we going to be silly goofy goobers together even if we're in public because who cares what people think? Are we going to give each other laughing attacks and keep adding on jokes to make each other giggle more? Are we going to go on wild little adventures that might get us into trouble but hey yolo so do it for the plot because why not? Are we going to take thousands of pics of each other like we're professional photographers and real life models? Are we both going to get into random tongue twisters while speaking in English then randomly switching to Spanish mid sentence? Are we both going to make every food we eat spicy because everything needs a little bit of spice to make it 10 times better even our own lives?
Is somebody gonna match my freak?

Are we going to bake together but I do everything and you just watch me and hand me stuff when I ask you for it? Are you gonna join me when I do my little dance if I'm enjoying my food? Are we gonna go to the beach and spend the whole day there because I don't wanna leave? Are you going to join me to get tattoos whenever I feel like I need to cope with something in my life or whenever we need extra adrenaline? Are you gonna hug me when I cry during sad movies or sad episodes of my favorite series? Are you gonna give me constant affection so I feel loved but also your attention so I feel cared for? I need someone that's going to match me now and match me again when I'm at my peak.

I want somebody, somebody who's gonna match me.

Is somebody gonna match my freak?

Rebirth of Style

She danced through the streets with such strong allure, every eye turned towards her, that was for sure.

She passed through the city in her dresses so bright, with colors that shimmered and fabrics that shined, spreading endless smiles and joy with all of her might.

Her outfits like a painting, the prettiest ever seen, proudly she wore her bold colors and prints.

But one day, something changed in her attire, no longer did she wear colors that inspire.

A change began to take its hold, my style a little less bright and a little more cold.

As I traded my pastels for darks and bold, switched my dresses for baggy jeans and sweats, gone were the soft fabrics that once adorned my silhouette.
No more skirts that would cause me disrespect

No more girly outfits that would bring me
regrets

Her wardrobe now dark, lacking any spark, her
once vibrant spirit seemed to be lost in the dark.

Many noticed and wondered at the
transformation, what could have caused this
sudden alteration?
Some said it was trends that had changed her so,
others thought it was simply time for her to
grow.

But deep down inside, she knew the truth, it
wasn't about fitting in or following youth. Her
new style reflected a fire within, a fierce
determination to be free and feel comfortable in
her skin.
So she walked through the streets with
confidence anew, a new sense of self, her
confidence again grew.

The change in my style speaks volumes you
view,
Of growth, resilience, and wisdom that blooms.
Well fashion is not just about what we wear, it's
the model of our souls laid bare.

Despite feeling physically safer and less at risk,

She no longer felt that inner self click
She missed the girl she used to be,
Long before she had to leave
She longed to break free from society's chains,
To embrace her true self, despite any disdain.

And slowly but surely, she found the courage
within, to dress as she pleased, to let her true
colors once again win.
So shine as much as the sun shines high in the
sky, and let your true essence never be shy.

With each new outfit, I feel more alive, my
confidence soaring as high as the sky.
No longer defined by others' gazes or trends, I
bloom like a flower that never bends

Now from lace, bohemian skirts to cargos and
crops my wardrobe tells a story, my crazy life
story in which my opinion is my priority.

Whatever I wear I feel like a beautiful pearl,

When posing in pictures I inevitably let out a
twirl because at the end of the day, I'm still just a
girl.

Forever a Wild Child

How am I supposed to act my age if I've never
been this age before?
People rush you to settle down, but there's still
so much more to explore

They say I should act my age, but why should I
conform and engage
in behavior that brings me no joy or rage?

I'd rather dance with joy like a child on stage,
life is too short to live in a compact cage, and
follow rules set by society's gauge.
I'll climb and run and skip hooray,
Unafraid of whatever society may think or say
I'll embrace my youth, no matter my age, and let
my spirit soar and rampage
I know laughter brightens up the day, in those
moments you look in my eyes, you see no
dismay,

For I am not bound by numbers on a page, I live
my life in a different way.

So I'm going to laugh and play,
giggle and yell yayyy as loud as I can

And whatever they say if you don't like it go on
with your day, let me be my own way
Running wild with wind in my hair, carrying
boundless energy beyond compare.

I am aware that time moves fast, but in my soul,
youth will forever be cast.
For age may come and wrinkles show, but deep
inside my spirit glows, with joy and wonder that
will never go, being forever young in the
afterglow.

So here's to not acting our age, and breaking free
from the mundane
Let's live, laugh, love, and turn the page

Sister Sanctuary

Each other's confidantes through thick and thin,
our sisterly love could get us through anything.

Even though life has brought us apart, when we
reunite our bond is reaffirmed, stronger than
ever

Through laughter and tears, we stand side by
side, facing life's challenges, we've always been
tight.

We lift each other up when one is feeling down,
we share each other's triumphs, a happiness
found.

From childhood days of laughter and play, to
adulthood's challenges that come our way,

We are sisters by chance, but friends by choice.

In times of need, we're always there for each
other
With open arms and hearts to care for one
another

Your wisdom guides me as I grow up.
All I have for you is gratitude and love
And although we aren't always near
I hope our bond will never dim or disappear.

Through the trials and triumphs we've faced, our
bond remains unbroken, tightly embraced. For
no matter how far we may roam or stray, us
sisters forever will find our way back.

Through life I'll continue to follow your lead,
you both are the parts of me I'll always need.

Chosen One

Everything she does she does with her heart in hand and her feet on the sand.
Guided by faith, she follows His plan, a promise of hope in a darkened land.

Her head's in the game she knows where to aim.
She walks with grace, creating her own pathway, her presence brightens up each day. A soul as golden as the sun, God's special girl, His chosen one.

The birds sing when she appears, for in her touch, they feel His grace, God's favorite girl, in every place.
With courage and strength, she faces each day, knowing that He will show her the way. God's favorite girl, a smile on her face.

She puts in her all, always does her best,
And no matter where she goes, she's always blessed.
God's always got her, that's her number one, he's the best,
She has no reason to fear, He tells her to get some rest,

Then the next day there might be a test,
But she knows as long as she believes,
She will continue to achieve.
In fields of flowers, she finds her peace, Her
laughter like a sweet release.
Her beauty lies not just skin deep, But in the
kindness that she keeps.
A light that shines for all to see, a symbol of
divinity, spreading love and joy without toxicity.
For in our hearts, we hold the key
To being God's favorite girl, you see.

Even if they are fallen down she will remain
upright, and if she ever goes down her spirit lifts
her again up high.
With every step, she spreads delight, A star in
the darkest night.
With eyes that sparkle like stars in the night, she
walks through this world with purpose and
might.
Embracing His love, spreading kindness and
light,
For in His eyes, we are all precious and bright.

The others question how she does it, they don't
understand, but how can she fall when she's got
her angels holding her hand?

She stands tall, For God's favorite girl will never
fall.

They only focus on the superficial, whatever to
them is beneficial and that is what's the issue
She is nothing like any of them,
A little princess fallen from heaven,
Wish for her when it's eleven eleven

So let us all strive to be like this pearl, to walk in
His light as God's favorite girl. Her heart filled
with love, no matter what she's endured. She
shines like a diamond, forever secure.
And like a diamond under pressure, she becomes
a greater treasure.